W9-AXG-238

Heroes for Young Readers

Written by Renee Taft Meloche
Illustrated by Bryan Pollard

Heroes of History for Young Readers

Written by Renee Taft Meloche
Illustrated by Bryan Pollard

*Heroes for Young Readers Activity Guides and audio CDs
are now available! See the back of this book for more information.*

For a free catalog of books and materials contact
YWAM Publishing, P.O. Box 55787, Seattle, WA 98155
1-800-922-2143 www.ywampublishing.com

HEROES FOR YOUNG READERS

AMY CARMICHAEL

Calvary at Village Green

Rescuing the Children

Written by Renee Taft Meloche
Illustrated by Bryan Pollard

YWAM
PUBLISHING
P.O. BOX 55787   SEATTLE, WA 98155

Amy Carmichael: Rescuing the Children   Text © 2002 by Renee Taft Meloche   Illustrations © 2002 by Bryan Pollard
Published by YWAM Publishing, P.O. Box 55787, Seattle, WA 98155   ISBN 978-1-57658-233-6   Printed in China.   All rights reserved.

More than a hundred years ago
       a little Irish lass
was sitting in a small tearoom
       next to a looking glass.

Her name was Amy Carmichael
       and she was having fun
enjoying tea and tiny cakes
       so tasty on her tongue,
when through the tearoom windowpane
       she noticed, in surprise,
a homeless girl was gazing in
       with hollow, hungry eyes.

She pressed against the window and
       her eyes peered at the plate,
which still was filled with sweet desserts
       that little Amy ate.

Since Amy's memory of that girl
just would not go away,
she wondered if God had a plan
for her to help some day.

Young Amy felt such deep concern
she scribbled out a note,
a promise to help children like
this girl, and so she wrote:
"When I am older, all grown up,
I know what I will do;
I'll build a safe and loving place
for little girls like you."

The years passed by and Amy grew,
    and often walked the streets,
inviting local children to
    her house so they could meet
to hear the Bible stories that
    she always loved to read,
and then she'd have them sing and clap
    to songs that she would lead.

One morning Amy visited
    the local Irish slums.
She passed out bread and Bible stories
    but felt overcome
by all the sights of poverty
    around her everywhere.
A blue-eyed girl caught Amy's eye—
    her ragged dress threadbare—
so Amy gave the girl some bread.
    She was so pale and small.
And then a stooped old woman with
    her head wrapped in a shawl
picked up the girl, and as the woman
    turned to walk away
the shawl fell from her face—and Amy
    gasped, surprised, dismayed.

The woman looked so worn and bent,
    but really was quite young!
And Amy soon discovered that
    this woman was among
the ones known as the "shawlies," those
    who covered up their heads,
not with warm hats—which cost too much—
    but with their shawls instead.

Now Amy felt such sorrow, she
    knew something must be done.
It wasn't long before she hatched
    a plan and had begun
to offer prayer and Bible study
    in her own church hall.
But many members of her church
    did not like this at all.

These shawlies, they told Amy, came
    with dirt and lice and fleas,
so bringing them inside their church
    made many feel displeased.

Yet Amy did not care what others
    thought that she should do.
She'd love and care for shawlies just
    as God would want her to.

Two years passed by, and Amy's work
    soon grew so big in size,
she had a larger building built
    where she could supervise
a weekly schedule that included
    singing, lunch, and band;
some Bible studies, prayer, and even
    sewing clubs were planned.

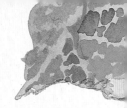

But things soon changed for Amy when
    her family had to go
to England where her work went on,
    but little did she know
that God had plans for her to work
    with those in other nations:
Japan, Ceylon, then India,
    her final destination.

Though it was hard to leave her family
    and the friends she'd known,
she knew that God was with her and
    she'd never be alone.

When she arrived in India,
    that country far away,
she learned that Hindus worshipped gods
    and idols every day.

Long silk and colored saris were
    the clothes rich women wore,
but Amy chose to dress in plain
    white cotton like the poor.

She told them about Jesus and
    the blessings He would send
if they would burn their idols and
    let Jesus be their friend.

Most Hindus disliked Amy and
    the Jesus that she knew,
for they did not believe the things
    that Christians know are true.

Yet one young girl named Arulai
    would sneak out of her home
to meet with Amy; she soon made
    the Christian God her own.

And when her family found this out,
    it caused a huge uproar;
they instantly forbade her to
    see Amy anymore.

But after eight months, Arulai
    was able to escape;
she ran to Amy's house, but in
    a very weakened state.

She lay in Amy's bed, so sick
    that she could barely speak.
Her father came to take her back
    but found she was too weak.

For many days he visited
and saw the love and care
that Amy gave his daughter when
he came to see her there.

And so, when she was finally well,
her father changed his mind,
allowing her to stay and live
with Amy all the time.

Another teenage Hindu girl
    decided she would be
a secret Christian and not tell
    her friends or family.

For if they knew that she believed
    in Christianity,
they'd beat her, and her very life
    might be in jeopardy.

But after three long years, she felt
    she somehow had to try
to find her way to Amy's house;
    she knew she lived nearby.

When evening came, the girl crept out
    and tiptoed through the night.
And as she crossed a bridge, a Christian
    banner came in sight.

That must be Amy's house, she thought,
    and pounded on the door.
And Amy took her in as she'd
    helped other girls before.

Now Hindu temple priests kept girls
        locked up both night and day.
They made the girls work just like slaves
        with no time left to play.

Right after one girl's father died,
        her weary mother said,
"You must live at the temple now.
        At least you will be fed."

The young girl's name was Preena; she
        was only five years old.
At night inside the temple she
        felt fearful, sad, and cold.

She never saw her mother and
        she could not play outside.
Since Preena wasn't loved at all
        she often hid and cried.

One night the girl escaped, but back
    at home her mother said:
"You cannot stay. You must return
    straight to your temple bed."

The Hindu priests then punished her
    to teach her to obey.
But Preena kept on dreaming she
    would one day get away.

Two years dragged on, and then one day
    she chanced to overhear
some talk about a woman who
    was said to live quite near:
her name was Amy and she traveled
    all throughout their land
to talk about the Son of God
    and offer helping hands.

She heard how kind this woman was
    and that she loved to give
her time, her self to children who
    had no good place to live.

So Preena thought, *If only I*
    could manage to get out…
Would Amy help me afterward?
    There was no time for doubt.

At night, so very quietly,
    she snuck out of her bed.
She tried the door. It was unlocked!
    So through the streets she fled.

She found a woman at a church
    and asked if she knew where
the Christian lady, Amy, lived
    and if she'd take her there.

Despite the danger, they set out
    and came to Amy's place.
They found her sipping English tea,
    a smile on her face,
so kind and warm that Preena felt
    at home and very safe.
She climbed right up in Amy's lap
    and into her embrace.

Now Amy kept this little child,
    who needed her a lot,
and Preena soon loved Jesus too
    and all the things He taught.

Some other temple children, then,
    were rescued, kept, and hidden,
though keeping even one of them
    was totally forbidden.

As Amy's family grew in size
    there wasn't room inside
the little house for all of them
    to live, and sleep, and hide.

She moved them to the country, to
     a village far away,
with houses and a nursery
     and land where they could play.

She also built a hospital
     so that it could provide
good care for all the orphans who
     would come from far and wide.

And Amy loved her children, she
        loved each and every one,
just as she once had promised when
        she was so very young.

Still, people all around the world
        are waiting everywhere:
the hungry, homeless, hurting ones
        who hope someone will care.

God's looking still today for those
        who'll follow where He leads
to reach out—just as Amy did—
        to those who are in need.

Christian Heroes: Then & Now

by Janet & Geoff Benge

Adoniram Judson: Bound for Burma
Amy Carmichael: Rescuer of Precious Gems
Betty Greene: Wings to Serve
Brother Andrew: God's Secret Agent
Cameron Townsend: Good News in Every Language
Clarence Jones: Mr. Radio
Corrie ten Boom: Keeper of the Angels' Den
Count Zinzendorf: Firstfruit
C. S. Lewis: Master Storyteller
C. T. Studd: No Retreat
David Bussau: Facing the World Head-on
David Livingstone: Africa's Trailblazer
Dietrich Bonhoeffer: In the Midst of Wickedness
D. L. Moody: Bringing Souls to Christ
Elisabeth Elliot: Joyful Surrender
Eric Liddell: Something Greater Than Gold
Florence Young: Mission Accomplished
Francis Asbury: Circuit Rider
George Müller: The Guardian of Bristol's Orphans
Gladys Aylward: The Adventure of a Lifetime
Hudson Taylor: Deep in the Heart of China
Ida Scudder: Healing Bodies, Touching Hearts
Isobel Kuhn: On the Roof of the World
Jacob DeShazer: Forgive Your Enemies
Jim Elliot: One Great Purpose
John Wesley: The World His Parish
John Williams: Messenger of Peace
Jonathan Goforth: An Open Door in China
Lillian Trasher: The Greatest Wonder in Egypt
Loren Cunningham: Into All the World
Lottie Moon: Giving Her All for China
Mary Slessor: Forward into Calabar
Nate Saint: On a Wing and a Prayer
Paul Brand: Helping Hands
Rachel Saint: A Star in the Jungle
Rowland Bingham: Into Africa's Interior
Samuel Zwemer: The Burden of Arabia
Sundar Singh: Footprints Over the Mountains
Wilfred Grenfell: Fisher of Men
William Booth: Soup, Soap, and Salvation
William Carey: Obliged to Go

Heroes for Young Readers and Heroes of History for Young Readers are based on the Christian Heroes: Then & Now and Heroes of History biographies by Janet & Geoff Benge. Don't miss out on these exciting, true adventures for ages 10 and up!

Heroes of History

by Janet & Geoff Benge

Abraham Lincoln: A New Birth of Freedom
Alan Shepard: Higher and Faster
Benjamin Franklin: Live Wire
Captain John Smith: A Foothold in the New World
Christopher Columbus: Across the Ocean Sea
Clara Barton: Courage under Fire
Daniel Boone: Frontiersman
Davy Crockett: Ever Westward
Douglas MacArthur: What Greater Honor
George Washington Carver: From Slave to Scientist
George Washington: True Patriot
Harriet Tubman: Freedombound
John Adams: Independence Forever
Laura Ingalls Wilder: A Storybook Life
Meriwether Lewis: Off the Edge of the Map
Milton Hershey: More Than Chocolate
Orville Wright: The Flyer
Ronald Reagan: Destiny at His Side
Theodore Roosevelt: An American Original
Thomas Edison: Inspiration and Hard Work
William Penn: Liberty and Justice for All

...and more coming soon. Unit Study Curriculum Guides are also available.

Heroes for Young Readers Activity Guides
Educational and Character-Building Lessons for Children

by Renee Taft Meloche

Heroes for Young Readers Activity Guide for Books 1–4
Gladys Aylward, Eric Liddell, Nate Saint, George Müller

Heroes for Young Readers Activity Guide for Books 5–8
Amy Carmichael, Corrie ten Boom, Mary Slessor, William Carey

Heroes for Young Readers Activity Guide for Books 9–12
Betty Greene, David Livingstone, Adoniram Judson, Hudson Taylor

Heroes for Young Readers Activity Guide for Books 13–16
Jim Elliot, Cameron Townsend, Jonathan Goforth, Lottie Moon

Heroes of History for Young Readers Activity Guide for Books 1–4
George Washington Carver, Meriwether Lewis, George Washington, Clara Barton

Designed to accompany the vibrant Heroes for Young Readers books, these fun-filled Activity Guides lead young children through a variety of character-building and educational activities. Pick and choose from the activities or follow the included thirteen-week syllabus. An audio CD with book readings, songs, and fun activity tracks is available for each Activity Guide.

For a free catalog of books and materials contact
YWAM Publishing, P.O. Box 55787, Seattle, WA 98155
1-800-922-2143 www.ywampublishing.com